THE SNOW APOCALYPSE: How to Prepare and Survive a Winter Storm

HAROLD M. HUNTER

Table of Contents

Introduction

It was a cold, dark night in the small town of Millville. The wind was howling and the snow was falling heavily, coating the streets and houses in a thick blanket of white. The residents of Millville were used to winter storms, but this one was particularly fierce.

As the night went on, the winds grew stronger and the snowfall became even heavier. The power lines started to sway and the branches of the trees snapped under the weight of the snow.

The town's emergency sirens blared, signaling for everyone to take cover. People rushed to gather their families and pets, and hurried to the safety of their basements.

As the storm raged on, the temperature dropped even further, causing the water pipes to freeze and burst. The town was left without running water and the residents were forced to rely on their emergency supplies.

The roads became impassable, making it impossible for emergency services to reach the town. The people of Millville were on their own, huddled together in the cold and darkness, waiting for the storm to pass.

The following morning, the sun finally rose and the storm began to subside. The residents emerged from their homes, surveying the damage left behind. The streets were covered in a thick layer of ice and the fallen tree branches made it difficult to navigate.

Many of the houses had suffered roof damage and some had even collapsed under the weight of the snow. The town was in a state of emergency and the people knew they had to work together to recover.

Over the next few days, the residents of Millville worked tirelessly to clear the streets and repair the damage caused by the storm. They used generators to power their homes and melted snow for drinking water.

As they worked, they learned more about the causes and effects of winter storms. They learned that these storms were caused by the collision of cold and warm air masses, and that they could be intensified by factors such as moisture and the earth's rotation.

They also learned that winter storms could have a number of impacts, including power outages, water shortages, and damage to infrastructure. They knew that it was important to be prepared for these storms, and to have emergency supplies on hand in case of a disaster.

The people of Millville learned a lot from that winter storm, and they were grateful to have survived it. They knew that they could handle whatever challenges came their way, as long as they worked together and stayed strong.

As they recovered from the storm, they took steps to ensure that they were better prepared for the future. They invested in snow plows and generators, and made sure to always have emergency supplies on hand.

Thanks to their efforts, the town of Millville was better equipped to handle winter storms in the future. And as they looked back on that dark, cold night, they knew that they had emerged stronger and more resilient than ever before.

Chapter One - What is a Winter Storm?

Winter storms can be a beautiful and majestic sight to behold, with snowflakes gently falling from the sky and blanketing the ground in a thick layer of white. But they can also be dangerous and destructive, bringing strong winds, icy roads, and power outages.

For those who live in areas prone to winter storms, it's important to be prepared and to know how to stay safe during these events. This book will provide a comprehensive introduction to winter storms, including their causes, impacts, and how to stay safe during and after the storm.

First, let's define what we mean by a winter storm. A winter storm is a type of low-pressure system that brings cold, wet, and often snowy weather to an area. These storms can be caused by a variety of factors, including the collision of cold and warm air masses, the movement of moist air over a cold surface, and the presence of a strong jet stream.

Winter storms can take many forms, from a light dusting of snow to a blizzard with near-zero visibility. Some common types of winter storms include snowstorms, ice storms, and nor'easters. Snowstorms bring heavy snowfall and strong winds, ice storms produce a coating of ice on surfaces, and nor'easters are a type of winter storm that commonly affects the northeastern United States and Canada, bringing strong winds and heavy precipitation.

The impacts of a winter storm can be wide-ranging and significant. Heavy snowfall can make roads and sidewalks treacherous, leading to traffic accidents and injuries. Icy conditions can cause power outages and damage to trees and power lines. Strong winds can cause damage to buildings and infrastructure, and can also lead to dangerous conditions on roads and waterways.

To stay safe during a winter storm, it's important to be prepared. This means having supplies on hand such as food, water, a flashlight, and extra batteries. It's also a good idea to have a plan in place for how to stay warm and safe in the event of a power outage. This may include having warm blankets and clothing, as well as a backup source of heat such as a fireplace or wood stove.

It's also important to stay informed about the storm and to follow any evacuation or shelter-in-place orders issued by authorities. This may mean staying tuned to local news and weather reports, or following the advice of emergency management officials.

In the aftermath of a winter storm, there are several things you can do to stay safe and begin the recovery process. This may include shoveling snow to clear paths, checking on neighbors and loved ones, and taking steps to prevent further damage to your home or property.

This book will delve deeper into these topics and provide more detailed information on how to prepare for and stay safe during a winter storm. It will also explore the science behind winter storms and discuss some of the ways in which we can mitigate their impacts.

Whether you're a seasoned veteran of winter storms or new to an area that experiences them, this book will provide

valuable information and guidance to
help you stay safe and informed during
the winter season.

Chapter Two - The Science Behind Winter Storms

Winter storms are a type of meteorological event characterized by low temperatures, strong winds, and precipitation in the form of snow, sleet, or freezing rain. These storms can range in intensity from a light dusting of snow to massive blizzards that can bring entire cities to a standstill. While they may be a nuisance for humans trying to go about their daily lives, winter storms are a natural and necessary part of the Earth's climate system. In this chapter, we will delve into the science behind winter storms, exploring the various factors that contribute to their formation and how they can impact our environment and communities.

One of the key drivers of winter storms is the temperature gradient between the polar regions and the equator. The Earth's atmosphere is divided into several layers, with the troposphere, which extends from the surface up to about 7-20 kilometers (4-12 miles) above the Earth's surface, being the layer in which we live and experience weather. The temperature of the troposphere decreases with altitude, with the coldest temperatures typically found at the top of the layer. This temperature gradient is caused by the absorption of solar radiation by the Earth's surface, which warms the lower atmosphere and drives the circulation of the Earth's atmosphere.

During the winter months, the polar regions receive less solar radiation due to their lower angle of incidence to the sun. As a result, the polar regions cool down significantly, leading to the development of a strong temperature gradient between the polar regions and the equator. This temperature gradient drives the circulation of the Earth's atmosphere, with cold, dry air sinking in the polar regions and warmer, moister air rising at the equator. This circulation is known as the "Hadley cell," and it plays a crucial role in shaping the Earth's climate.

The circulation of the Earth's atmosphere also drives the movement of air masses, which are large bodies of air that have similar temperature and humidity characteristics. Air masses form over large landmasses or bodies of water, and they can be classified as either polar, tropical, or arctic based on their temperature and humidity characteristics. When an air mass moves from a region of lower pressure to a region of higher pressure, it can result in the development of a winter storm.

The formation of a winter storm typically begins with the development of an area of low pressure, known as a cyclone, over the polar regions. As the cyclone moves southward, it brings with it cold, dry air from the polar regions. As this cold air encounters warmer, moister air at lower latitudes, it can lead to the development of clouds and precipitation. The type of precipitation that forms depends on the temperature of the air and the ground. If the air is cold and the ground is warm, the precipitation may fall as rain. If the air is cold and the ground is also cold, the precipitation may fall as snow or sleet. If the air is above freezing but the ground is below freezing, the precipitation may fall as freezing rain.

The intensity of a winter storm is influenced by several factors, including the temperature gradient between the polar regions and the equator, the strength of the cyclone, and the availability of moisture. The stronger the temperature gradient and the stronger the cyclone, the more intense the winter storm is likely to be. Similarly, the availability of moisture is an important factor in the intensity of a winter storm. If there is a lot of moisture available, the storm is likely to produce more precipitation.

Winter storms can have significant impacts on our environment and communities. They can cause power outages, damage infrastructure, and disrupt transportation.

Chapter Three - Impacts of Winter Storms

Winter storms can have significant impacts on both natural and human systems. These impacts can be physical, economic, and social in nature, and can have long-lasting effects.

One of the most significant impacts of winter storms is on transportation. Snow, ice, and freezing temperatures can make roads and highways treacherous, leading to accidents and delays. Air travel can also be disrupted by winter storms, with flights being cancelled or delayed. This can have major economic consequences, as businesses and individuals may be unable to get where they need to go, leading to lost productivity and revenue.

Winter storms can also have significant impacts on infrastructure. High winds, heavy snow, and freezing temperatures can all take a toll on buildings and other structures. Roofs can collapse under the weight of heavy snow, and pipes can freeze and burst due to the cold. These types of damage can be costly to repair, and can disrupt essential services such as power, water, and telecommunications.

In addition to the physical impacts, winter storms can also have social and psychological effects. Prolonged periods of cold and darkness can lead to feelings of isolation and depression, especially for those who are elderly or otherwise vulnerable. Winter storms can also place a strain on emergency services, as they may be called upon to respond to a greater number of accidents and other incidents.

One of the most serious impacts of winter storms is on human health. Cold temperatures can cause hypothermia and frostbite, and snow and ice can make it difficult for people to get around, leading to slips, falls, and other injuries. Winter storms can also disrupt the supply of food and other necessities, leading to shortages and higher prices.

Another impact of winter storms is on the natural environment. Heavy snowfall can alter the landscape, causing erosion and landslides. Cold temperatures can kill plants and animals, especially those that are not adapted to survive in such conditions. Winter storms can also disrupt the migration patterns of certain species, leading to population declines.

Despite the many negative impacts of winter storms, it is important to note that they also have some benefits. Snow and ice can act as insulators, helping to protect plants and animals from extreme temperatures. Winter storms can also replenish water supplies, as snow and ice melt and run off into rivers and streams.

In conclusion, winter storms can have a range of impacts on both natural and human systems. These impacts can be physical, economic, and social in nature, and can have long-lasting effects. It is important to be prepared for winter storms and to take steps to minimize their negative impacts as much as possible. This can include having an emergency kit on hand, staying informed about weather conditions, and following the advice of authorities when a winter storm is forecast.

Chapter Four - Preparing for Winter Storms

Winter storms can be dangerous and disruptive, so it is important to be prepared for them. Here are some steps you can take to ensure that you and your loved ones are safe during a winter storm:

1. Know your risk

Different areas have different levels of risk for winter storms. It is important to be aware of the type of winter storms that are common in your area and how to prepare for them.

2. Make an emergency kit

Having an emergency kit on hand can be a lifesaver during a winter storm. Your kit should include items such as non-perishable food, water, flashlights, a battery-powered radio, extra batteries, a first aid kit, warm clothing, blankets, and any necessary medications.

3. Keep your car winter-ready

If you live in an area where winter storms are common, it is important to make sure your car is prepared for the winter weather. Keep your car's gas tank full, as it will help to keep the fuel line from freezing. Make sure your tires have enough tread and are properly inflated, as this will help with traction on snow and ice. Keep a winter emergency kit in your car as well, including items such as blankets, warm clothing, a flashlight, and a small shovel.

4. Know how to stay warm

During a winter storm, it is important to stay warm to avoid hypothermia and frostbite. Wear layers of loose, warm clothing and make sure your head, hands, and feet are covered. Stay inside if possible, and if you must go outside, try to limit your time outdoors.

5. Keep your home winter-ready

Winterize your home by sealing any drafts and adding insulation to help keep heat in. Keep your thermostat set to a consistent temperature, as large fluctuations can cause pipes to freeze. If you will be away from home during a winter storm, make sure to shut off your water and drain your pipes to prevent them from freezing.

6. Stay informed

Make sure to stay informed about the latest weather conditions and any emergency alerts. Keep a battery-powered radio on hand and tune in to local news stations for updates. Follow your local emergency management agency on social media or sign up for their alerts.

7. Have a plan

It is important to have a plan in place in case you lose power or need to evacuate during a winter storm. Make sure everyone in your household knows what to do and where to go in case of an emergency.

By following these steps, you can help to ensure that you and your loved ones are prepared for winter storms and stay safe during this dangerous time of year.

Chapter Five - Winter Storms Around the World

Winter storms can be a major inconvenience and can cause significant damage, especially when they strike areas that are not used to dealing with such severe weather. These storms can take many forms and can occur in many different parts of the world, each with its own unique characteristics and impacts.

Here, we will explore the various types of winter storms that occur around the world and how they can affect the people and communities they impact.

Blizzards

Blizzards are a type of winter storm that is characterized by strong winds and heavy snowfall. These storms can occur in a variety of locations, but they are most common in the mid-latitudes, where cold air from the polar regions can collide with warm, moist air from the tropics. In the United States, blizzards are most common in the Midwest and Northeast regions, although they can also occur in other parts of the country.

Blizzards can be extremely dangerous, as the combination of strong winds and heavy snowfall can lead to poor visibility and treacherous driving conditions. They can also cause power outages and damage to infrastructure, such as roads and buildings. In extreme cases, blizzards can lead to stranded vehicles, hypothermia, and other serious health issues.

To prepare for a blizzard, it is important to have an emergency kit on hand that includes warm clothing, non-perishable food, and other supplies. It is also a good idea to have a plan in place for how to stay safe during the storm, such as finding shelter and staying off the roads.

Ice Storms

An ice storm is a type of winter storm that occurs when rain or freezing rain falls and then freezes on contact with cold surfaces, such as roads, sidewalks, and trees. These storms can be particularly dangerous because the ice that accumulates can make it difficult to walk or drive and can also cause damage to trees and power lines.

Ice storms are most common in areas that have relatively mild winters, as the presence of cold surfaces is necessary for the rain to freeze. In the United States, ice storms are most common in the Midwest, Great Plains, and Northeast regions.

To prepare for an ice storm, it is important to have an emergency kit on hand and to be prepared for possible power outages. It is also a good idea to have a plan in place for how to stay safe during the storm, such as avoiding travel if possible and staying indoors.

Snowstorms

A snowstorm is a type of winter storm that is characterized by heavy snowfall. Snowstorms can occur in a variety of locations, but they are most common in areas that experience cold winters, such as the mid-latitudes and high latitudes. In the United States, snowstorms are most common in the Midwest, Northeast, and Rocky Mountain regions.

Snowstorms can be dangerous because the heavy snowfall can make it difficult to travel and can cause damage to infrastructure, such as roads and buildings. They can also lead to power outages and other problems.

To prepare for a snowstorm, it is important to have an emergency kit on hand and to be prepared for possible power outages. It is also a good idea to have a plan in place for how to stay safe during the storm, such as finding shelter and staying off the roads.

Winter Cyclones

A winter cyclone is a type of winter storm that is characterized by strong winds and heavy snowfall. These storms can occur in a variety of locations, but they are most common in the mid-latitudes, where cold air from the polar regions can collide with warm, moist air from the tropics. In the United States, winter cyclones are most common in the Midwest and Northeast regions.

Chapter Six - Climate Change and Winter Storms

Climate change refers to the long-term warming of the planet, which is largely caused by human activities such as burning fossil fuels and deforestation. Winter storms, on the other hand, are severe weather events that can bring snow, ice, and strong winds to a region during the winter months.

While the relationship between climate change and winter storms may seem somewhat indirect, the two phenomena are actually closely linked. Rising global temperatures are leading to more frequent and severe winter storms in many parts of the world. Here's how:

Warmer air can hold more moisture, which can lead to heavier snowfall during winter storms. When cold air masses collide with warmer, moist air, the result is often a winter storm with heavy snowfall. As the planet warms, the air is able to hold more moisture, leading to heavier snowfall during winter storms.

Climate change can alter wind patterns, leading to more severe winter storms. The earth's atmosphere is a complex system, and even small changes in one part of the system can have far-reaching effects. As the planet warms, it can alter wind patterns, leading to more severe winter storms. For example, a warming Arctic region could lead to a shift in the jet stream, which could bring more extreme winter weather to parts of the northern United States and Europe.

Melting sea ice can lead to more powerful winter storms. Sea ice acts as a buffer, protecting coastlines from the full force of winter storms. As the planet warms and sea ice melts, coastlines become more vulnerable to the impact of winter storms. In addition, the open water left behind by melting sea ice absorbs more heat from the sun, which can further fuel the development of winter storms.

Rising sea levels can increase the risk of flooding during winter storms. Climate change is causing sea levels to rise, which can increase the risk of flooding during winter storms. When a winter storm coincides with high tides, the combination can lead to serious flooding in coastal areas. In addition, the higher sea levels can make it more difficult for stormwater to drain away, leading to further flooding.

Warmer temperatures can lead to more frequent winter storms. While it may seem counterintuitive, warmer temperatures can actually lead to more frequent winter storms. As the planet warms, it can create more favorable conditions for the development of winter storms. For example, warmer temperatures can lead to more atmospheric instability, which can fuel the development of winter storms.

In conclusion, the link between climate change and winter storms is complex and multifaceted. Rising global temperatures are leading to more frequent and severe winter storms in many parts of the world, and this trend is likely to continue in the coming decades. It is important that we take action to mitigate climate change and reduce our carbon emissions in order to protect ourselves and future generations from the worst impacts of these storms.

Conclusion

Winter storms can be serious and dangerous events that can have a significant impact on individuals, communities, and entire regions. In order to prepare for and survive a winter storm, it is important to take the necessary steps beforehand to ensure that you and your loved ones are safe and well-equipped to handle the challenges that may arise.

The first step in preparing for a winter storm is to gather essential supplies and create an emergency kit. This should include non-perishable food, water, medications, blankets, warm clothing, and other essentials. It is also a good idea to have a backup source of heat, such as a wood stove or fireplace, in case of a power outage.

Next, it is important to familiarize yourself with the types of winter storms that are common in your area, as well as the specific hazards that they may pose. For example, if you live in an area that is prone to blizzards, you should be prepared for heavy snowfall and strong winds that can make travel difficult or impossible. If you live in an area that is prone to ice storms, you should be prepared for slippery roads and power outages.

In the event that a winter storm is imminent, it is important to stay informed about its progress and any emergency alerts or evacuation orders that may be issued. This can be done through local news sources, weather forecasts, and emergency notification systems. It is also a good idea to have a plan in place for how you will communicate with loved ones and how you will access essential services in the event of a winter storm.

During the winter storm, it is important to stay warm and dry. This means staying inside as much as possible and limiting your exposure to the cold and wet conditions. If you must go outside, be sure to wear warm, waterproof clothing and cover as much of your skin as possible. It is also a good idea to keep a supply of non-perishable food and water on hand in case you become stranded or unable to access supplies.

If you are stranded in your car during a winter storm, it is important to stay with your vehicle and try to keep it running if possible. This will help to keep you warm and provide a source of heat. If you are unable to keep your car running, wrap yourself in blankets and use your emergency kit to stay warm and hydrated.

After the winter storm has passed, it is important to take the necessary steps to clean up and repair any damage that may have occurred. This may include shoveling snow, repairing roofs or windows, and cleaning up debris. It is also a good idea to check on your neighbors and offer assistance if needed.

In conclusion, preparing for and surviving a winter storm requires careful planning and the ability to adapt to changing conditions. By gathering essential supplies, staying informed about the storm and any emergency alerts, and taking steps to stay warm and safe, you can increase your chances of surviving a winter storm and minimize the impact it has on you and your loved ones.